Amgueddfa Genedlaethol Cymru
National Museum of Wales
Cardiff 1989

Welsh Industrial Workers Housing 1775~1875

by Jeremy Lowe
Welsh School of Architecture, UWIST, Cardiff

Acknowledgements:
Photographs: 9, David Anderson; 14, Crown Copyright, reproduced by permission of the Controller of Her Majesty's Stationery Office; 17, National Museum of Wales; 55, Port Talbot Historical Society; the remaining photographs were taken by the author. Maps and Plans: 49, 51, 53, 54, 61, 62, redrawn from the First Edition of the 1:2500 Ordnance Survey; 14, Royal Commission on Ancient and Historical Monuments in Wales; 33, Bernard Morris FRICS; 13, 23, 39, 44, 59, Welsh School of Architecture; the remainder are by the author.

The author wishes to thank David Anderson for supplying transcriptions of the 1841 Census Returns and for help with the surveying of houses, Chris Powell for similar help, David G. Jones for information on slate quarry workers' housing, Bernard Morris for Swansea housing, and also the staffs of the National Library of Wales and the Glamorgan, Gwent and Gwynedd Archive Services, Arthur Rees (Port Talbot Historical Society), Peter Smith (Royal Commission), the County Planning Officer, Clwyd County Council, Brian Lingard and Partners and the many house owners and occupiers for their essential contributions to this booklet.

Drawing Scale:
The plans and sections of individual houses are all reproduced to a scale of 1:250 (10mm represents 2.5m). The diagrams of housing layouts are not drawn to a standard scale.

Note: There is no right of access to any of the houses illustrated in this booklet. Many of the buildings have already been demolished. In a few cases, as mentioned in the text, there is an expectation that public opening will eventually be possible.

Introduction

This booklet illustrates buildings which until recently were thought to be just a commonplace background to everyday life. It is not a history of industrial housing in Wales – that has yet to be written – but it does try to link the variety of house form which can (or rather, could) be seen in our towns with the conditions of life experienced by our ancestors. After this introduction, there are five sections in the booklet, each dealing with one aspect of the development of house design.

Since men first specialised in the production of stone axes and flint implements there have been manufacturing industries in Britain, but with rare exceptions the scale of manufacture was small until the middle of the eighteenth century. Unless he lived over, or next to, his place of work, the home of an industrial craftsman was scarcely different from the ordinary dwellings of crofters and cottagers. The character of industrial workers' housing changed when individual craft work began to be replaced by the factory system, one of the features of the Industrial Revolution. New technology, the greater use of water and steam power, and changes in the organisation of business, made possible the continuous employment of fifty or a hundred workers where only a few years before there had been ten or twenty. The dwellings of these people, built in groups near the sites of industry, are easily recognised as a new form of housing.

Growth in some of the industries of late eighteenth and early nineteenth century Wales was very rapid. In the South-East, iron production expanded enormously, using local ores and coal; slate quarrying developed in the North-West and woollen textile manufacture in Mid-Wales, while in the North-East coal mining, metal production and textile industries were all to be found. The prosperity of mining for copper, lead and zinc, which were found in several parts of Wales, fluctuated, but at many mines there were periods of great expansion. Thus it is possible to find throughout Wales industrial communities which came into existence between 1775 and 1825. Many were in remote localities where there had been only a few scattered farms, and where the building of houses was as necessary as the sinking of shafts or the construction of furnaces. Key workmen had to be attracted to fill essential jobs, while accommodation was also needed for the many labourers.

The siting of houses was dictated at first by industrial convenience; they had to be within walking distance of the occupants' places of work. The designs used were governed only by the wishes of the industrialists, who were subject to no regulation from authority. Most houses provided little other than shelter and a means of heating and cooking, with perhaps some storage for food. The number of rooms varied normally between two and four; houses with only one room, or with five or more, were uncommon, though not unknown. Sanitation was primitive; many houses had none, and the others were provided only with a privy set over a cess-pit, usually shared between several households. Overflows and seepage from such pits, and water running off the waste-strewn land around the works and houses, frequently polluted the wells and streams which were the only source of drinking and washing water.

These insanitary conditions were common throughout industrial Britain in the early nineteenth century, but they could not be tolerated for ever. In 1833 cholera joined the dreadful list of fevers and other diseases already recurrent in the larger towns. Its arrival helped to stimulate public action, under powers given first by local Sanitary Acts, and then with the Public Health Act of 1848 by general regulation. Even so the first Act which applied controls to all housing throughout Britain was not passed until 1875, though local regulations of some sort were in force in many places before that date. Thus housing for the coal-mining industry of South Wales, which was mostly developed after 1850, is built to considerably better standards than the earlier ironworks housing nearby.

In most British towns the houses built in the unregulated phases of the Industrial Revolution have now been cleared away. Many were demolished long ago during the rebuilding of town centres, and more recently slum clearances have taken the remainder. But in Wales circumstances have favoured the survival of early housing. The tide of industry which flowed up the valleys onto the high moorlands often receded rapidly, leaving many settlements isolated. One cause of this recession was the improvement of land and sea transport, which helped the diversion of Welsh raw materials to larger manufacturing centres on the coast or in England, or the import of overseas materials as a complete substitute.

This left the metal-mining towns of the North-East and of Mid-Wales, and the iron towns of the South-East without any industrial purpose. Even the wool weaving of Newtown and Llanidloes was transferred elsewhere. Some of the more remote settlements were abandoned, but most of the original industrial towns maintained a depressed existence, in which little redevelopment of housing was possible. In the North-West the slate towns began to decline about 1900; in Mid-Wales the weaving towns altered little after 1880, and several of the iron towns of the South-East were already in recession in 1860. The coal industry took in some part of the iron-working labour force, but it too has been in decline since 1920. Of course, great efforts have been made recently to bring new industry into these depressed areas, but for a long time the pace of domestic change was still slow. Until the early 1970s it was possible to find unaltered examples of the unregulated houses of the first industrial phase, but modern policies of clearance and improvement will soon bring such opportunities to an end.

This booklet is therefore a record of houses that can be seen no longer and a guide to those that will remain only in reconstructed form. Most of the illustrations are recent, because it is rare to find old photographs or drawings that show clearly houses which can be identified today as significant examples of early design. In any case a photograph taken in 1880 or 1900 does not always give a more faithful picture of a house built in, say, 1810 than does one taken recently. Most of the photographs are accompanied by a drawn plan and cross-section, showing the original form of the house. There are only two interior scenes. Early views taken inside Welsh industrial workers' houses are extremely rare, and it is scarcely possible today to find interiors in their pre-1875 condition. The selection covers the whole country, but necessarily there are more examples from places where many early houses are known to have survived, and fewer from towns where redevelopment took place some time ago.

Housing built after 1875, predominantly in the big industrial centres of South and North-East Wales, has not been included.

Materials and Methods of Construction
Most building materials are so heavy or come in such large sizes that transport is a major factor in the cost of the finished work. Before bulk carriage systems were developed, each district of Wales had its own tradition of house-building, using local materials. These traditional methods produced solid, durable farmhouses and barns, many of which still survive, and much less substantial cottages, with rough walls and light thatched roofs. Many of the early industrial houses draw more on the farmhouse methods than on those used for the cottages; they are well-built, differing from the farmhouses only in a few imported details.

As the Industrial Revolution progressed and the size and value of industrial businesses increased, housing costs became more significant, and durability seemed less important. Some houses were built on land leased

for as little as 21 years. Economy was sought in cheaper materials, lower transport costs and reductions in the need for skilled craftsmanship. The opening of the Glamorganshire Canal in 1794 allowed builders in Merthyr Tydfil to roof houses with slates brought by ship from North Wales to Cardiff; in the Rhymni valley, only four miles away, where there was no canal, the traditional stone slabs were still being used in 1830, even though they required heavier roof timbers and more skill in fixing. Skilled carpentry in local hardwood was replaced by simpler construction in imported machine-sawn softwood, and components such as windows were made to standard designs in workshops, instead of being made up on the site for each house.

Local materials continued in use for wall construction for some time. Despite the skilled work involved, quarrymen's houses were built of waste slabs from the slate quarries (*page 43*) and iron workers' houses of sandstone from the iron ore mines. In 1850 the tax on bricks was lifted, at the same time as the railway network was growing. Bricks were easier to lay than stones, and gradually replaced them, first in the expensive parts of walls (the jambs and heads of window and door openings and the quoins at the corners of a building) and then eventually throughout. By 1875 the last traces of traditional building were disappearing from Wales.

The Influence of 'Polite' Architecture
Economic pressures were not the only influence on house design; ideas of order and method, spreading at a time of growing scientific and social awareness, also had their effect. During the eighteenth century most rural labourers, in Wales as elsewhere in Britain, lived in the rough cottages mentioned earlier. But a few landowners, while improving their estates, did build better houses which gradually became known to writers on rural affairs.

About 1770, one of the best known travel writers of the day observed that the houses of the common people in the Lleyn peninsula were "very mean, made with clay, thatched and destitute of chiminies". (*Tours in Wales* by Thomas Pennant, first published 1773; 1810 ed. 2, 386). In 1775, an expert who advised the landed gentry on the management of their estates, wrote that the state of "the shattered hovels which half the poor of this kingdom are obliged to put up with, is truly affecting to a heart fraught with humanity". (*Hints to Gentlemen of Landed Property* by Nathaniel Kent, first published 1775; 1793 ed. 207). Kent published drawings, of houses like some already built for improver landowners, which provided the three rooms he thought necessary for a labourer's family. So fashionable an architect as John Wood, designer of the Royal Crescent at Bath, produced a book of new designs for labourers' houses in 1781.

Though it was a long time before the ideas of these men were fully accepted, the influence of 'polite' society upon design was strong. The broad irregular proportions apparent in traditional building steadily gave way to symmetry and upright shapes. Formal architectural ideas were introduced, from a simple rhythm of windows (*page 30*) to a grand composition (*page 40*); ornamental facades were applied in both classical and romantic styles (*pages 38 and 43*). Older houses were remodelled to give more height inside and a more 'polite' exterior; the influence of fashion continues in the same way today, as alterations made to meet current ideas of good taste, change or wholly obliterate the original character of old houses.

Elevation of two Bricked Cottages of the largest Size with Hipped Ends.

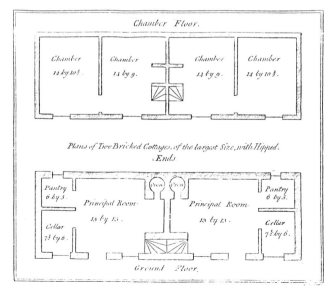

Chamber Floor.

Plans of Two Bricked Cottages of the largest Size, with Hipped Ends

Ground Floor.

A Design from Nathaniel Kent's *Hints to Gentlemen of Landed Property* first published in 1775.

Interior Fittings, Finishes and Furniture

Since the early industrial houses were without any internal water supply or sanitation the only original interior fittings that survive are the fireplaces and the larder and fuel stores. In the South-East, larders were generally large, up to 2.5 square metres in area, with a stone slab and two timber shelves, and ventilated by a separate window. Elsewhere they were often less satisfactory; in Newtown (Powys), for example, back-to-back houses had no more than a cupboard ventilated into the living room.

In mining districts, unsaleable small coal was available in plenty. No fuel stores were provided, but frequently there are three fireplaces in a four-roomed house. In Mid-Wales houses fuel was often kept in a coal-hole below the stairs. The living-room fireplace itself is usually the principal fitting left in an early house. Originally these fireplaces had a massive open hearth spanned by a heavy lintel or arch; in later years cast-iron ranges were almost invariably installed, as in this example at **10 Union Court, Crescent Street, Newtown** (Powys). The damage where the right side of the opening was cut back for the oven shows that the range here is an insertion, but it is possible that the iron crane, from which cooking pots could be hung over the fire, is an original feature, dating from about 1835-40. Some houses were originally provided with brick ovens (*page 37*), but these were uneconomical to fire, and eventually gave way to communal bake-houses which, with brew-houses and wash-houses, were shared by all the households in a court, row or part of a street.

In outlying districts, and even in some parts of towns, people had no access at all to any form of sanitation; often as a last resort, "the cinder heaps . . . are frequented by persons of all ages and sexes, who manage the best way they can." (*Report on the State of Bristol, . . . Merthyr Tydfil and Brecon* by Sir Henry de la Beche, London, 1845, 80). Many other households had only the shared use of a privy, which not surprisingly, was often in bad repair and very unpleasant. Indifference to sanitary needs continued throughout the first industrial age in Wales. About 1850 when asked why none of the Blaenavon Iron and Coal Company's cottages was provided with water closets, a principal agent of the company said that "they were of no use and if constructed the people would not use them". (T. Dyne Steel. reprinted in *Pontypool and District Review*, 11, October 1972).

Little can be seen today of the original interior finishes and furnishings of early industrial houses, but it is clear that they were often very primitive. The walls were rough plastered, or even simply bare brick or stone; every

year or so they were whitewashed, gradually building up a thick multi-layered coating. The floors were flagstoned, or just made of rammed earth, sometimes surfaced with pebbles or pitched stonework.

Furniture was rudimentary, often no more than a collection of boards and boxes. The most fortunate and provident couples might acquire new furniture at the time of their marriage, but even they had to be content with a roughly carpentered bedstead, a table, a few stools, perhaps a chair and a chest for clothing, all of which had then to last a lifetime. Many households had only some of these items and those at second or third hand. From the mid-century, chairs became more common though sleeping accommodation was still frequently over-crowded. Gradually the insides of houses began to assume a more recognisable air of homeliness, with sack or rag mats on the floors, curtains at the windows, a shelf or two of decorated china and a few ornaments with the candleholders on the mantleshelf.

The location of this Mid-Wales barrack dwelling (*see page 10*) has not been identified, but though taken in 1901 it typifies the living conditions of several decades earlier. On the left are beds, each shared by two men, standing on a wooden staging below which the occupants' private belongings could be stored. On the other side of the fireplace the miners or quarrymen took their meals at a plain table. They had no chairs, but sat on wooden forms or on the lids of provision tubs which can be seen half-hidden under the table. The walls are covered with scenes of action in the South African War, cut from the popular illustrated papers. One or two of these are peeling away from the wall, which is tell-tale evidence of the ill-ventilated, humid atmosphere in a low room where clothes were often hanging up to dry.

Traditional Houses in Industrial Settings

Some of the earliest industrial houses in Wales show clearly their relationship with rural dwellings. During the first phase of the Industrial Revolution, many factory masters had to attend personally to all aspects of their business and could spare little time for the designing of houses. They left the decisions about plan shapes and constructional methods to local builders, familiar with the traditional practices of the district. The industrial nature of such houses is shown mainly by the way they were grouped. Most industry was still organised on a very small scale, so that a works settlement may contain only some ten to twenty houses, usually arranged in one or more rows.

14-21 Gellideg, Merthyr Tydfil (Glamorgan) *SO 0345 0675* is near the site of the Cyfarthfa furnaces, which dated back to 1769. The lower end of the row is the oldest part; it was built as a farmhouse, probably before the start of the ironworks. Three successive additions were then made, which changed the row from a rural building to an industrial one. The last addition at the upper end (*left*) was built before 1813. Each house in this part has two ground floor rooms and a larder, with a large sleeping room above which would have been undivided when the houses were first built. The oak roof structure is still like that of rural buildings, and like them would have been covered originally by stone slabs. In the distance can be seen Cyfarthfa Castle, built by the third Crawshay ironmaster in 1825.

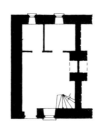

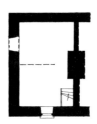

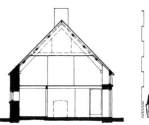

Ground Floor   First Floor   Cross Section

Stack Square and Engine Row, Blaenavon
(Gwent) *SO 2500 0923* are part of one of the
earliest industrial settlements to be seen in
Wales. The two parallel rows of houses are
joined by a third range of building which, in the
early nineteenth century, contained the
company shop and perhaps the offices of the
proprietors. The whole group was built between
1789 and 1792, at the same time as the first
two Blaenavon furnaces, which are only 100
metres away.

The houses have a conventional plan, with two
rooms on each floor, and a larder; their
construction is quite traditional too, with stone
walls outside and oak beams and partitions
inside. By the standards of their time they are
quite large, varying from 57 square metres at
the ends of the upper row to 44 square metres
in the lower row. Even the smaller size is above
average. This suggests that the houses were
built for the foremen and craftsmen, who were
employed on full-time contracts because they
were essential to the working of the furnaces.
Though derelict in 1971, when this picture was
taken, Stack Square and Engine Row are to be
restored eventually as part of the Blaenavon
industrial monument.

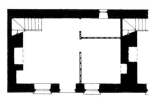

Ground Floor

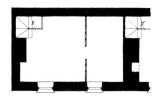

First Floor

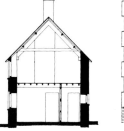

Cross Section

In the West and North of Wales many one-storey houses with two rooms were built by peasant farmers and farm workers during the century from 1750 to 1850. The same type of house, often built in blocks of three, was widely adopted for industrial dwellings throughout the West. In mining and quarrying areas some of these two-room buildings were not family houses, but barracks, used from Monday night to Friday night by men who lived too far away to make a daily journey to work.

In **Cwmystwyth** (Dyfed) one of the oldest and largest lead mines in Wales was partly mechanised in 1785. Even so there was only a gradual change in the way of life of the miners, who lived in scattered crofts and cottages, working on the land as well as in the mine. **Penybryn** *SN 8292 7535* the earliest Cwmystwyth houses that are recognisably industrial, were built about 1835, high up the valley beyond the upper limit of the workings. There were two blocks built end-to-end, each containing three houses. By 1974 one had collapsed and the other was roofless. Each single-storey house had a kitchen and a separate sleeping chamber, over which a *croglofft* gave extra sleeping space. The roof was supported on pinewood poles roughly squared, but bolted together with long wrought-iron bolts.

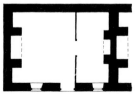

Ground Floor

Cross Section

Near the ruins of the **Drws-y-Coed** copper mine in **Dyffryn Nantlle** (Gwynedd) *SH 542 534 & SH 546 536* are several short rows of houses. **Bwthyn** (*photo*) which is still occupied, is at the end of a row of three houses exactly the same size on plan as the three survivors at Penybryn, (*opposite*). Behind and nearer to the rock-face is another row, similar in size and form, but now a roofless ruin (*drawing*). The mine was already working in the 1790s, but these two rows were probably not built until after the Napoleonic War, though certainly before 1836. It is likely that both rows were intended for use as barracks; the dwellings each have two rooms, almost equal in area, but no *croglofft*.

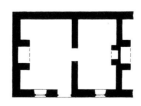

Ground Floor

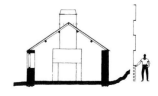

Cross Section

New Designs for Industrial Workers

Though many works proprietors were satisfied at first with the traditional forms of Welsh housing, in other parts of Britain new house types were being developed towards the end of the eighteenth century especially to suit the needs of industry. Some of these designs were introduced to Wales by industrialists who either had used them already elsewhere or hoped that they would help to reduce construction costs and save land. The new designs used less building material, and often economised by combining workshops and dwellings in one block or by placing houses back-to-back, one over another, or in interlocking layouts.

Bunkers Hill, Bersham (Clwyd) *SJ 3120 4926* was built soon after 1785. It is one of the earliest rows of industrial houses in Wales. At first sight, these single-storey two-room dwellings are similar to the traditional cottages of the West (*page 10*). But the design was actually imported from Shropshire, where it was then common, by the English ironmaster John Wilkinson. The unbroken long row of houses built end to end, the brick walls and the steeply-pitched roof, better suited to clay tiles than to Welsh slates, are all features found in early housing in the Shropshire coal-field. Bunkers Hill, which can only be visited by prior appointment, was derelict and unused in 1976.

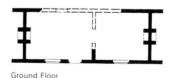

Ground Floor

Cross Section

In the textile-working towns of Mid-Wales many rows of houses were surmounted by open workshop floors or Factory Rooms, housing the hand-worked looms on which Welsh flannel was woven. Traditionally the craftsman's workshop was part of, or next to, his house; the Factory Room adapted this tradition to the needs of the weaving industry, by bringing together under one roof the craftsmen who worked for one master. It also increased the use made of the land and the building structure.

1-4 Union Street, Penygloddfa, Newtown (Powys) *SO 1065 9196* is a late example of this type of building. The row of tiny two-room houses, with the elegant doorcases typical of many houses in Newtown, is surmounted by one long room for flannel looms. The fireplaces are arranged to avoid any obstruction of this room. The row was built between 1835 and 1841, when hand-loom weaving was becoming obsolete, and the once prosperous workers were willing to rent smaller and smaller houses. The lean-to extension at the back was added many years later.

Ground Floor

First Floor

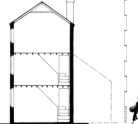

Back-to-back housing was developed in the English Midlands and in Yorkshire. Each block contained two separate rows of dwellings, separated by a thin 'spine' wall. This layout allowed more houses to be packed onto valuable sites in fast growing towns and made maximum use of materials. Many tens of thousands of back-to-back houses were built in English towns after 1790 and use of the design soon spread to Wales. Then about 1830 the idea developed that poor ventilation could be one of the causes of epidemic disease. Back-to-backs had no through ventilation (from front to back) and so eventually new developments of this type were prohibited.

21-25 Ladywell Street, Newtown (Powys) *SO 1085 9144* were built about 1810 for workers in the woollen industry. This 3-storey block contained six back-to-back houses, three facing into the street and three into **Welsh Court** at the back, with two larger houses (24 and 25) beyond. Each back-to-back had one room per floor, with a small larder below the stairs. The timber-framed construction, at this late date infilled with bricks laid on edge, was traditional in many parts of Britain and remained in use in Mid-Wales up to a relatively recent times. But even in Newtown, plain brick, which was more solid and durable, became the usual material by about 1820. Already in this building the lowest part of the wall was built in solid brickwork. Elsewhere in Britain, the once numerous timber-framed back-to-backs were demolished long ago. These houses, which survived until 1966, were probably some of the last to go.

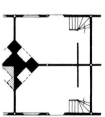

Ground Floor

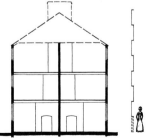

Cross Section

In the iron-working districts, back-to-back housing was relatively uncommon. The first settlements were often scattered, so that it was not necessary to economise in the use of land. But the back-to-back layout also saved building materials, which is probably why it was chosen for **Bunkers Row, Blaenavon** (Gwent) *SO 2521 0943*. This row was built on open hillside, the first section (latterly Nos. 1-10) being completed about 1792, at the same time as Stack Square (*page 9*). It provided twenty small houses for the lower-paid workers; each house had a single room at ground level and a loft above, reached by a ladder. These houses too may have been an English design, but nothing of the kind now survives in English towns. In Blaenavon, their inadequacy was recognised before 1814, when blocks of detached larders were added on both sides of the row. Then about 1860 the houses, which would otherwise have been demolished, were rebuilt with higher outside walls, a new roof and first floor, and larger doors and windows. Later still each back-to-back pair was converted into one house, in which form the row survived until 1972.

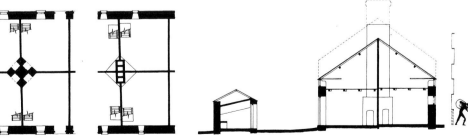

Ground Floor   First Floor   Cross Section

Another innovation tried out in the period 1790 to 1840 was the 'dual' row, in which one range of houses formed the basement for an entirely separate range above. This design was well-suited to sloping sites, common enough in the industrial areas of South Wales. The row was placed along the slope with the doorways of the upper houses at ground level on the uphill side and of the lower houses on the other, downhill side. Usually the lower houses had only one storey but on very steep slopes two could sometimes be fitted in. The dual row must not be confused with the later hillside design found throughout Wales, which also has three floors on the downhill side, and two on the uphill side, but all as part of the same house.

One of the earliest dual rows was built at **Nantyglo** (Gwent) between 1793 and 1795. **Office Row** SO 1925 1055 provided all the houses required for labourers and craftsmen in an ironworks built in those years under the direction of Harford and Company, merchant bankers of Bristol. Similar houses were built at Sunnybank, Melingriffith, near Cardiff, where the firm had an interest in the tin plate works. In Office Row the eighteen upper houses had four rooms and a larder, while the basement houses, much overgrown in this 1961 view, had two rooms and a larder excavated into the hillside. The basement was solidly built, with semi-circular vaults over each room to provide a good foundation for the house above. The front of Office Row can be seen clearly in the watercolour drawing of Nantyglo ironworks (*right*) which was made about 1827.

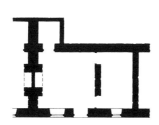

Lower House

Upper House

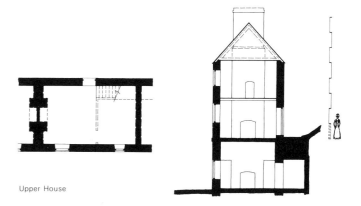

"Some time ago I visited a poor woman in distress, the wife of a labouring man: she had been confined only a few days, and herself and infant were lying on straw in a vault through the outer cellar, with a clay floor impervious to water. There was no light or ventilation in it, and the air was dreadful. I had to walk on bricks across the floor to reach her bedside as the floor itself was flooded with stagnant water." Mr. Holmes, speaking of a Liverpool dwelling, to the Commissioners Inquiring into the State of Large Towns and Populous Districts, 1845.

In Wales, cellar dwellings never presented so great a problem as they did in cities like Liverpool, where 40,000 people were so housed in 1840. True cellars, with their floors entirely below ground level, were not common in Welsh towns, for the lower ranges of dual rows, though built back-to-earth on one side, were usually open to ground level at the other. This apparent improvement made it easier for the authorities to overlook the failings of the dual row. Mr. James, Chairman of the Merthyr Tydfil Board of Poor Law Guardians, stated in 1845 that in his district these dwellings were "tolerably well-lighted and provided with fireplaces". But in truth the lower houses, like true cellars, were prone to dampness and lacked through ventilation.

The accuracy of Mr. James' opinion can be tested by looking at one of the last of the dual rows, **65-73 Plymouth Street, Merthyr Tydfil** (Glamorgan) *SO 0537 0546* which was built about the time that he made his statement. There were five upper houses in this row, and four basements, all numbered separately in the street sequence. The upper houses had two rooms, with a very low ceiling in the bedroom. The basement houses had just one square room, with a door to the street, a window, a fireplace, and a cupboard recess; the partitions between one house and another were lightly built, so that they could be altered easily. These dreadful habitations were scarcely high enough inside for a man to stand upright. A floor of flagstones laid on plain timber boards and joists separated them from the upper houses. There was just 1.75 metres headroom under the boards, and no more than 1.43 metres under the central beam. The floor level was three steps below the street; when the row was surveyed in 1970, water covered the floor to a depth of several centimetres. This extraordinary row survived until 1972, at least sixty years after its lower houses had been evacuated.

Sir Henry de la Beche, who examined Merthyr Tydfil in 1845 for the Health of Towns Commission, thought that the worst part of the town was near Pont Storehouse, where 1500 people lived in an area known as The Cellars. "Though so named," he wrote, "they are not cellars, but a collection of small houses of two stories, situated in a depression between a line of road (Bethesda Street) and a cinder-heap . . . The space between these houses is generally very limited; an open, stinking and nearly stagnant gutter, into which the house refuse is, as usual, flung, moves slowly before the doors. It is a labryrinth of miserable tenements and filth, filled with people, many of whom bear the worst characters. The rents of these houses seem to vary from 3s to 5s per month. One house was found to measure 10 feet (3.0m) by 5 feet (1.5m) and 6 feet (1.8m) high in the lower room, and 10 feet by 5 feet, 5 feet high in one place sloping to 1 foot 6 inches (460mm) opposite in the upper room. There was a tenement of only one room, 7 feet (2.1m) by 4 feet 6 inches (1.4m), 5 feet 3 inches (1.7m) high, with a bed in it, and a stinking gutter partly under the floor. The generality of the houses are, however, of larger dimensions."

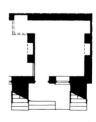

Lower House

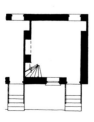

Upper House

First Floor

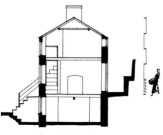

Cross Section

Instead of constructing back-to-back or dual rows, some builders sought economy by interlocking the rooms of adjacent houses. Such forms also seem to have had their origins in the English Midlands. They did not play much part in Welsh industrial housing, occurring only on isolated sites.

Butlers Row, Abersychan (Gwent) *SO 2658 0318* was built about 1825 to an interlocking design found also in the Shropshire coal-field. The houses were arranged in pairs, with one larger and one smaller room on each floor. The smaller rooms were placed side-by-side, one lit from the front and one from the back of the row. There were no other windows or doors in the back wall. The Z-shaped partition separating the two houses was built of timber filled with bricks laid on edge, only 110mm thick including its plaster finish. This view was taken in 1972 shortly before the row was demolished.

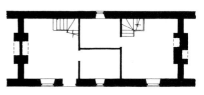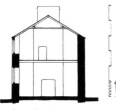

Ground Floor   First Floor   Cross Section

Halton High Barracks, Chirk (Clwyd) *SJ 2965 4007* was built early in the nineteenth century, to house miners who worked in nearby pits. Here two rows of differing height were built back-to-back and so interlocked that each house had four rooms plus an extra room in the attic on the top floor of the downhill block. The first, third and fourth attic windows (from the left of the picture) light the rooms which are reached from the houses in the back row. The attic rooms may possibly have been intended for lodgers; some industrialists insisted that their family tenants should also take in lodgers when necessary. Though these buildings were photographed in 1976, the coal pits for whose workers they were built had closed before 1838, an early example of the ebbing of the industrial tide.

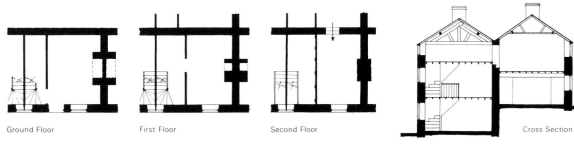

Ground Floor   First Floor   Second Floor   Cross Section

Experiments and Variations in Design

Many different types of houses were built in Wales during the first four decades of the nineteenth century. Some of these designs were bad, below any reasonable minimum standard of accommodation; others showed varying degrees of ingenuity and foresight. The progress towards satisfactory types was hesitant and slow, probably because it was difficult for builders to exchange information and experience. The pattern books upon which many depended for their ideas paid little attention to working-class housing; it is clear too, that some builders, perhaps most, worked by 'rule of thumb' without using drawings of the design they were constructing. In such a situation useful ideas would have spread mainly by personal contact.

6-13 Nantygwenith Lane, Georgetown, Merthyr Tydfil (Glamorgan) *SO 0430 0639* was otherwise known as Gregory's Row, but it is not known if this is the name of its builder or its owner; they may have been the same person. These two-room houses were built about 1841. Though small in area, they show some refinement in planning when compared with other two-room houses. Opposite the fireplace in the main room there is a substantial larder (lacking the window it ought to have had) and a bed-recess which, having its own window, could be curtained off completely from the living space. Seventy years before Nathaniel Kent had written that "it is shocking . . . that the wife should have no private place to be brought to bed in". Gregory's Row pays some attention to the realities of childbirth and parenthood.

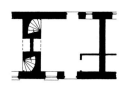

Ground Floor

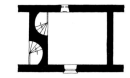

First Floor

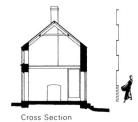

Cross Section

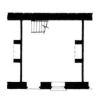

Ground Floor

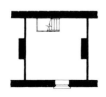

First Floor

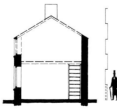

Cross Section

In the big towns of Wales, as in England, almost all the earliest workers' housing was demolished long ago. A chance survival of the early growth of **Cardiff** is **Jones Court,** off **Womanby Street,** *SO 1809 7638* a row of two-room houses long ago converted to store rooms. They were built before 1840, when Cardiff had fewer than 10,000 inhabitants, far less than either Swansea or Merthyr Tydfil. Many owners of sites in the town developed such cheap courtyards at that time. They were bad houses, packed closely together on narrow plots behind the street frontage, with cess-pit privies shared between several householders, and no water supply other than the public water-pumps, whose sources were often contaminated. Jones Court, having survived so long, may now be preserved as a row of small shops.

The use of back-to-back housing to keep down construction costs was a common feature of building practice in the textile-working towns of Mid-Wales, especially in Newtown (Powys), where a number of such blocks were used as a satisfactorily wide foundation for one or two floors of workshop space. Narrow passageways through the ground floor of each block gave access from the street to the back row and also to the other houses and workrooms which were built around the enclosed back yard or court. Though large in size, the back-to-back block was often lightly constructed, only its outside walls being more than a half brick in thickness.

6-9 Union Street, Penygloddfa, Newtown (Powys) *SO 1069 9198* was a building particularly grim in appearance. The houses in this short row formed the lower part of a factory built between 1830 and 1833 by John Matthews (c1785-1846), a flannel manufacturer; there were eleven houses in all, one fronting onto Crescent Street for Matthews' own occupation, and these ten back-to-backs in Union Street. Over them were two floors of factory space and a roof loft for storing materials. In Matthews Court, reached through the arched passageway, there was a short row of three smaller houses and some other out-buildings, including the 'necessaries' (*privies*) whose use was shared by all the occupants prepared to keep them 'in a wholesome condition'. There was also a pump in the court, though just where is not known.

The main building was constructed in two stages, the further four houses (*two in this picture and two facing Matthews Court*) and the workshops above them being an addition, built before 1833 and called the 'New Factory'. The two factory spaces had separate access; the original part was reached by climbing two flights of timber stairs rising from the doorway at the right of the picture, while the stairs to the New Factory started from Matthews Court. Eight of the ten houses had two rooms. They were about the same in plan area as the older houses in Ladywell Street, Newtown (*page 14*), but the ceilings were higher and the windows larger. Each house had a timber cupboard larder with a grille above its door ventilating it into the main living room. There was a coal-hole under each flight of stairs. At the nearer end of the New Factory were two houses slightly larger in area and each having two upstairs rooms, but otherwise the same fittings as the other houses.

John Matthews' factory was demolished in 1974; a similar building, but fitted with elegant doorcases, has been preserved a few yards away in Commercial Street, where it now houses the Newtown Textile Museum.

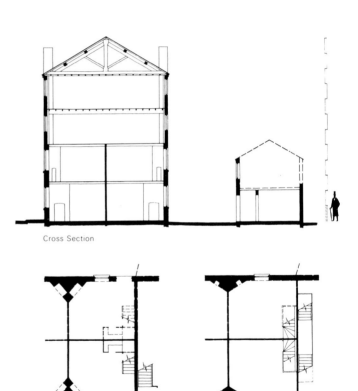

Cross Section

Ground Floor

First Floor

The use of bed recesses, or of cupboard or box beds, might give a married couple some degree of privacy, but a better solution was to provide two sleeping rooms, as Nathaniel Kent had recommended in 1775. Unfortunately, a two-storey three-room house is difficult to design, simply because there must be an unequal number of rooms on each floor.

The designer of these houses at **2-5 Chapel Street, Penygloddfa, Newtown** (Powys) *SO 1078 9192* chose a simple answer to the three-room problem; he built back-to-back dwellings of normal size (almost identical with those in Union Street, *page 24*), but then partitioned the upstairs room into two. Each half of the upper floor had its own window; notice how the iron casements (a common industrial detail in the district) are partly disguised to look like 'polite' sash windows. This picture also shows how building was developed sequentially along a street frontage. The earliest part is the manufacturer's house at the bottom of the hill, with its workshop on the top floor. Next came the first four back-to-backs, also with a workshop above. A little while later another four were added, leaving a narrow passage as the only access to the back houses. The builder took considerable care over the setting-out of the window and door openings on this difficult sloping site, and also included well-built brick arches and projecting eaves in his design.

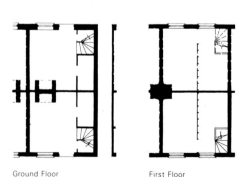

Ground Floor

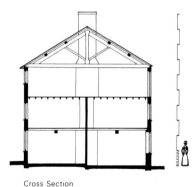

First Floor

Cross Section

The Crawshay family, owners and managers of the Cyfarthfa and Ynysfach ironworks at **Merthyr Tydfil** (Glamorgan), had many three-room houses built to their own special design. This row is at **Rhydycar** *SO 0487 0547* on the west bank of the disused Glamorganshire canal. They were built before 1813, perhaps for Richard Crawshay, founder of the dynasty, who died in 1810. Each house is a complete two-room dwelling with an extra bedroom and a larder added at the back in an 'outshot' which is covered by the long 'catslide' roof slope. Structurally this is a clumsy design with unnecessarily thick internal walling and heavy roof timbers supporting the catslide. Yet it was widely used around the Crawshay works from 1795 to 1830, and may have been introduced to Wales by the family. Similar houses, but with the upstairs room divided, were used by the proprietors of the Plymouth Works at Merthyr Tydfil up to 1820.

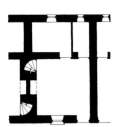

Ground Floor

First Floor

Cross Section

At Dowlais (Glamorgan) two types of three-room house were tried out. Before 1825 a small number of double-fronted houses were constructed, similar to the four-room design (*page 9*), but with an undivided upper floor lit by one window over the central doorway. After 1825 many more three-room houses were built to the design illustrated here.

28-33 Pond Street, Dowlais (Glamorgan) *SO 0718 0786* were built probably about 1840. They had one room downstairs, fitted with a wall-cupboard which served as a larder, and two rooms upstairs which were separated only by a light timber partition. There was a fireplace in the back room upstairs. Notice also the rounded front of the house at the right which stands at the junction of the streets. This feature was quite characteristic of housing in Dowlais.

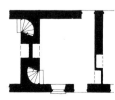

Ground Floor

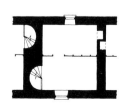

First Floor

Cross Section

Upper New Rank, Blaenavon (Gwent) *SO 2445 0963* was built about 1825. These houses were typical examples of the first Blaenavon Company's most important design. In all the Company constructed about 225 such houses, of which 72 were to slightly larger preliminary designs. All had the same layout of kitchen and back bedroom on the ground floor with the large open sleeping room above. This layout was more efficient in its use of materials than the Crawshay house (*page 28*), while providing better interior conditions too. Design refinements included the sealing and insulation of the underside of the roof, and the unusual arrangement of window openings. It is likely that this house type was developed from traditional sources, such as the Gellideg row at Merthyr Tydfil (*page 8*). The houses at the Varteg Forge, near Blaenavon (*page 48*), which were built in 1804, show a half-way stage in this evolution.

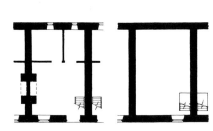

Ground Floor

First Floor

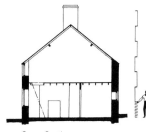

Cross Section

The three-room house was intended for a supposedly 'typical' family, the married couple with dependent children. The Census Returns from 1841 onwards show that such families made up only a relatively small proportion of the households in an industrial area, and that the others varied greatly in size and composition. Many householders, including some of the parents who had to support several young children, took in lodgers to supplement the family income. Of course as children grew up, they tended to move away, but even in large families many stayed in the home contributing to the joint income until they were married. Some remained with their parents even after marriage, while those who were widowed and left with young children might return to their family home. As a result many households included middle-aged or elderly people, young adults and adolescents, and small children. The three-room house could not be adequate for such a diversity of age, sex and family relationship.

It is often difficult to link the 1841 Census with particular houses but the returns do show who actually lived in the Upper New Rank at Blaenavon. This diagram is one way of comparing the different households. Each column represents one house. Adult residents, over 15 years old, and juveniles of 8 to 14 years, are each indicated by a square in the column; the letters in the squares show their occupations, in capitals for adults and in small letters for juveniles. Children under 7 years old are represented by a half square. Men and boys are identified by upright letters or solid circles, women and girls by italic letters or open circles. Squares above the line show the householder's immediate family, those below the line the other relatives or lodgers.

The diagram shows that only four or five of the twenty households fit the so-called typical pattern; another half dozen consist of a married couple living with adult children. The other households all include lodgers, the sixth and fifteenth in the diagram being particularly varied in age, sex and relationship. One married couple were evidently keeping a lodging house. It should not be thought that this range of occupancies was in any way exceptional. In the adjacent Lower New Rank, household size varied between two, an ironstone miner and his wife, and thirteen, which was the number of people recorded in two houses, while in a third house there lived two complete families and three lodgers, totalling ten adults and two juveniles.

Householder's Family

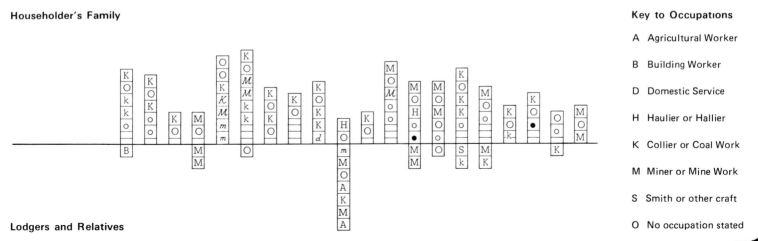

Lodgers and Relatives

Key to Occupations

A Agricultural Worker

B Building Worker

D Domestic Service

H Haulier or Hallier

K Collier or Coal Work

M Miner or Mine Work

S Smith or other craft

O No occupation stated

The problem of decency, which was so important to the critics of two-room and three-room houses, was avoided (at least in theory) by the four-room design. Separate sleeping areas could be provided for parents and children of both sexes. In 1833 John Claudius Loudon, then the foremost authority on working men's housing, said that the four-room house showed a "cheap and simple mode of building dwellings of the lowest degree of accommodation". Single-fronted houses of this type, with rooms back and front on each floor, can be found all over Wales, with internal arrangements that vary from place to place.

8-13 Foundry Road, Abersychan (Gwent) *SO 2650 0335* were built between 1824 and 1826 in association with Hunt Brothers' Pentwyn Furnaces. The houses were demolished in 1972. They had the semi-circular stone stair typical of South-East Wales, placed so that the upstairs back room could be reached only by passing through the larger front room. There were no back doors. The smaller room downstairs was the marital bedroom, not a scullery or back-kitchen. In better-planned houses this room is rather bigger and usually has its own fireplace. The block was built on rising ground with a continuous sloping roof line, a detail of design that later became a characteristic feature of Welsh working-class housing.

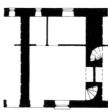

Ground Floor

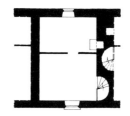

First Floor

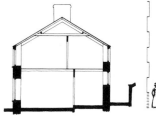

Cross Section

5-14 Princess Street, Swansea (Glamorgan) *SN 6530 9275* were built between 1830 and 1837. These four-room houses had straight timber stairs, rising directly from the street doorway to both upper rooms. The back room downstairs could have been a back-kitchen or a bedroom. It was probably partitioned off from the space leading to the back door, part of which would also have been used as the larder. The longer rear roof slope and the thick internal wall suggest that these houses were related to the Merthyr Tydfil 'catslide outshot' type (*page 28*). The wall which separates two rooms of one house is much thicker than the wall between two houses at ground floor level.

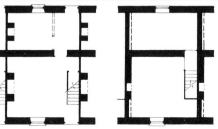

Ground Floor   First Floor

Cross Section

Ground Floor

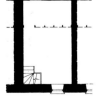

First Floor

Cross Section

Brickfield Terrace, Machynlleth (Powys) *SH 7448 0094* is a row of 10 four-room houses; the house at the near end is slightly larger, and carries a date stone reading "Brickfield Terrace, M. Jones, 1826". At Machynlleth the wool cloth industry still employed many cottage outworkers, who carried out several processes in their own houses and also worked on the land in summer. The layout of the houses in Brickfield Terrace, and in other nearby row in **Heol-y-Doll**, probably reflects this tradition. The main room was a workroom. Food was cooked at its fireplace, but other domestic tasks were carried out in the back room, which is lit only by the outside door and cannot have been a bedroom.

In most districts a few houses were built with more than four rooms (there were as many as seven in Plantation Row, Ebbw Vale). These larger dwellings were intended for chargehands and foremen, whose status and privileges were carefully preserved.

2-4 Brake Road, Brymbo (Clwyd) *SJ 2905 5360* is a block of five-room houses, built to an English Midland design with a timber stair rising from the corner of the main room along the back wall. The Brymbo ironworks was set up by John Wilkinson, one of the Bersham partners (*page 12*), who bought the estate in 1793, but 2-4 Brake Road was built after his death in 1808; there is a date stone (now partly defaced) on the gable wall, which can be read as "1815". These houses are generously proportioned and were once solidly constructed, though now they have been damaged by subsidence; the use of the Midlands design shows how much the industrial builders of North-East Wales continued to be influenced by English practice.

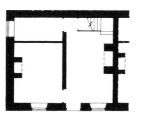

Ground Floor

First Floor

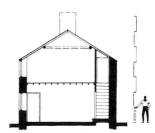

Cross Section

Builders and Occupiers

The form of an industrial house can tell us something about the motives of its builder and his relation to its occupants. Many of the early factory masters sought to influence all aspects of the lives of their workpeople, even outside working hours. Some built on an impressive scale either from genuine concern for their workers, or as a conscious exercise in 'image-promotion'. Other masters showed their influence in a less benevolent way, providing housing which was a constant reminder of the workman's state of dependence.

Cyfarthfa Row, Georgetown, Merthyr Tydfil (Glamorgan) *SO 0438 0658* shows the later development of the common four-room double-fronted house of South-East Wales. There are actually two parallel rows, totalling fifty houses, separated by short gardens. They were built when the sole owner of the Cyfarthfa Iron Works was William Crawshay the Younger; one house, at the North-West end, carries a date stone for 1840, the year after the Chartist march on Newport. By the standards of the day these houses were generous in size and well built, which suggests that whatever his view of the Chartist movement, William Crawshay saw the merit of providing better housing for his workforce. Cyfarthfa Row is to be modernised internally and preserved.

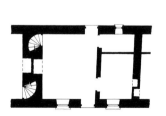

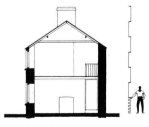

Ground Floor   Cross Section

Bayliss Row, Nantyglo (Gwent) *SO 1934 1016*
preserves the names of Joseph and Crawshay
Bailey, cousins of William Crawshay and
masters of the Nantyglo and Beaufort ironworks.
Crawshay Bailey had an almost legendary
reputation as an autocratic, tight-fisted
employer, which is reinforced by the existence
at Nantyglo of several rows of minute two-room
houses, smaller than any others of their date in
Gwent. Bayliss Row was built about 1827 on the
hillside opposite the ironmaster's house. The
status of master and man is made clear by the
original orientation of the row, with all windows
and doors on the inward-facing, uphill, side of
the row. The present windows on the outward
side, which would have directly overlooked
Bailey's house and gardens, were not inserted
until he had moved his home elsewhere.

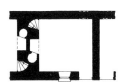

Ground Floor

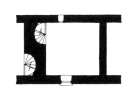

First Floor

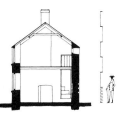

Cross Section

Victoria Avenue, Llanidloes (Powys) *SO 9567 8478* was built between 1832 and 1840 as a part of Pryse's Wool Factory. The long row of houses forms the 'polite' public facade of the whole factory group, intended to give a good impression to the outside world. It is built to a typical 'pattern-book' design, in good brickwork with well-proportioned sash windows and carefully detailed doorcases, which give an elegant appearance to what was in reality only an ordinary row of two-room back-to-back houses with attic workrooms above. The archway leads into a yard bounded by the mill buildings and the back facade of the houses, both of which are entirely industrial in character, built of rough stonework with wide arched casement windows. The houses have now been 'cut through', making each pair of back-to-backs into one good house, but the whole character of the front facade will be lost if more of the windows are replaced by modern single-pane sashes.

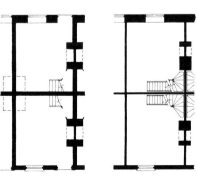

Ground Floor   First Floor   Cross Section

Ground Floor   First Floor

Cross Section

Middle Row, Butetown, near **Rhymni** (Glamorgan)
SO 1042 0915 is part of an iron-works built between
1825 and 1830 for the Marquess of Bute. This powerful
landowner was willing to spend money upon the
appearance of his property. His furnaces were Egyptian in
style and his workers' houses are robustly Palladian. The
three rows are made up of two-storey houses with four
rooms, attics, and in one row, basements; the centre
three-storey blocks may once have provided 'barrack'
rooms for single men. Butetown is now a conservation
area. Its design was probably based on a planned village at
Lowther in Cumbria, which was begun in 1765 by the
architect James Adam.

The Ranks, Abercarn (Gwent) *ST 2155 9496* formed another model settlement, of 56 four-room houses arranged in four identical closely spaced rows on the east bank of the Crumlin Branch of the Monmouthshire Canal. It was built between 1847 and 1850 for the Abercarn and Gythen Colliery. In this design the practicalities of public health absorbed all the attention which at Butetown (*opposite*) was given to appearance. In the paving of streets and the provision of sewers and refuse receptacles, the Ranks were well advanced. Otherwise the house design was solid but inflexible; all the rooms were the same size, lit by identical cast-iron windows. The row layout provided no gardens nor any variety in the spaces formed by the buildings. The lowest row has now been demolished, and the others are unlikely to survive long.

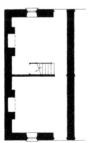

Ground Floor

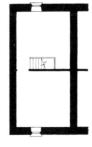

First Floor

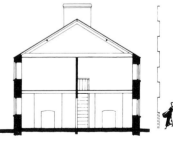

Cross Section

Chapel Row, Blaenavon (Gwent) *SO 2441 0924* was a late and correspondingly large example of the 'isolated' row, built in 1839 by the Blaenavon Iron and Coal Company. The manager of this firm used up much of its resources on new buildings until the inevitable cash crisis curtailed his schemes in 1840. He favoured a classical style of building – the great Balance Arch at Blaenavon Works also dates from this time. Between the two halves of the row there was once a massive chapel in the same classical style. Behind the row vast deposits of furnace slag built up in the later nineteenth century. At many Welsh ironworks land for tipping became so scarce that whole rows of houses were abandoned to be buried in slag. Ten of the houses at the far end of Chapel Row were destroyed in this way about 1910; the others survived until 1971, but nothing at all can be seen today.

Ground Floor

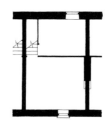

First Floor

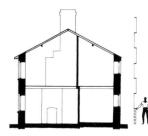

Cross Section

In the late eighteenth century landed proprietors with a taste for 'Picturesque' design began to ornament their country estates with pretty Gothick cottages. The industrialist living amidst the squalor created by his own activities was usually less worried about appearances, but nonetheless some housing of this kind was built. The promoter of this row of slate-quarrymen's houses is, as yet, unknown but they obviously respond to romantic ideas about design.

They were built, probably about 1860-65, just to the north of the **Aberllefenni Slate Quarry**, near **Corris** (Gwynedd) *SH 7674 1037*, and are now in the last stages of dereliction. Only the front was ornamented with Tudor-style slate drip-mouldings and traceried sashes and fanlights. It had no practical purpose, being invisible from every possible public viewpoint. The houses were solid but primitive, constructed from slate slabs and roughly-cut floor and roof timbers. The layout of the plan was clumsy with an awkward access from the stairs to the main bedroom; on the ground floor the lean-to scullery was apparently an afterthought, though probably built at the same time as the rest of the house.

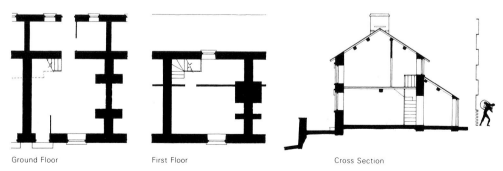

Ground Floor　　　　First Floor　　　　Cross Section

Those who chose house-building as an investment were not all wealthy men. Speculative development was often on a small scale yet still might overstretch the developer's resources. Nor were all developers individuals; before widespread share ownership was made possible by the Limited Liability Acts of 1855-62 and popularised by the railway companies, many friendly societies and charitable bodies invested their funds in housing, and used the rents as their source of income.

Wesley Cottages, Pontrhydygroes (Dyfed) *SN 7397 7247* were built right at the end of the period covered by this booklet. They stand next to Capel Bethel which was erected in 1874; the cottages were built shortly afterwards, according to local tradition by the 'captain' of the Grogwinion lead mine which was then in full production. Like many similar houses in the Ystwyth valley, Wesley Cottages are simple, even old-fashioned in design, but generous in size with four good rooms, and showing the benefit of a period of exceptional prosperity in lead mining. They are an obvious improvement over such earlier houses as Penybryn (*page 10*). But in 1875 lead mining in Wales, faced by competition from richer foreign ores, was about to slide into decline and eventual extinction. As has happened so often, the most obvious relics of a vanished industry are the houses of its workers and the chapel that they built.

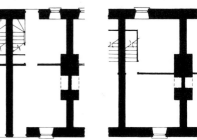

Ground Floor   First Floor

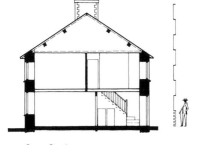

Cross Section

Rhes Fawr, or **New Street, Deiniolen** (Gwynedd)
SH 5792 6308 is part of a speculative development begun
between 1832 and 1838 by David Griffith of Llanfagdolen.
The houses, intended for workers in the Dinorwic Slate
Quarries, had only two rooms; the rear annexes are of
later date. There were fourteen houses facing New Street
and another similar row behind facing undeveloped land.
In 1868 a local historian wrote that David Griffith ''began
building about forty houses (*sic*) without first sitting down
and thinking about the task he had to complete''. (D.M.
Jones and J. Roberts *Traethodau ar Waen Gynfi,* trans.
D.G. Jones). As a result ''he fell into the trap of temptation
even to the point of banishment'', that is his creditors
pursued him into exile.

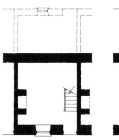

Ground Floor

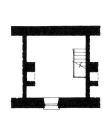

First Floor

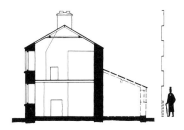

Cross Section

Most of the houses illustrated so far were built by industrialists, or by other people seeking an investment. But some skilled workmen earned and saved enough to be able to buy a home. A few could raise money on their own, or by joining in partnership with relatives, while an increasing number became householders by forming small building societies in which the members pooled their savings and, sometimes, their spare time too.

40, Percy Street, Garndiffaith (Gwent) *SO 2628 0464* was a substantial four-room house constructed about 1844 in a settlement where many sites had already been developed by colliers and iron-workers. Often such a man would build two houses, with the help of a small mortgage; he would live in one and use the rent received for the other to help pay off the mortgage. This particular house though was a single unit, added back-to-back to an earlier dwelling. It was sold in February 1845 to a collier, Henry Powell, and his sister. The variations in the size and shape of the stones used in the wall show that material was obtained from several sources in small amounts. This house was demolished in 1971 and its site is no longer visible. The lady in the picture is Mrs Powell, the last occupant of the house and creator of the tiny, well-tended garden.

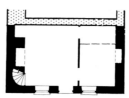

Ground Floor

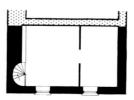

First Floor

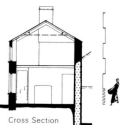

Cross Section

Club Row, Abersychan (Gwent) *SO 2662 0355* was constructed before 1841 by the Pentwyn Benefit Building Society, founded in 1838. This was a terminating society, which was dissolved once all the houses had been finished and paid for. It built about thirty houses in three rows around a small triangular green. All were of the four-room double-fronted type with a distinctive arched doorway. The walls are soundly built outside, but the internal partitions were rather irregular, showing perhaps that members who were less well skilled could still give their labour to the society. Most of the Pentwyn Society houses have been demolished, but Club Row was still in good condition in 1976.

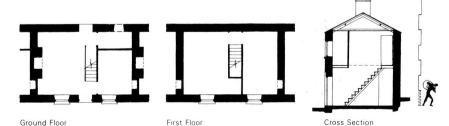

Ground Floor　　　　First Floor　　　　Cross Section

47

The Grouping of Industrial Houses

The needs of defence or the location of markets, which had so strong an influence upon medieval settlement, played no part in the siting of the first industrial towns. No one could forsee how much a settlement might expand, and some places grew rapidly with scarcely any control at all. Merthyr Tydfil, with its four large ironworks, developed between 1760 and 1800 from a remote village into the most populous town in Wales. By 1803 it was still in a state of 'scattered confusion', its irregular streets built piecemeal without order or plan, though a start was then being made on the setting-out of proper street lines. In other places, where only one or two industrialists were in charge a simple form of site planning was sometimes adopted. But usually the predominant ideas were that houses should be built close to places of work, and as quickly and cheaply as seemed reasonable.

Forge Row, Cwmavon near **Pontypool** (Gwent) *SO 2704 0654* is a single-row settlement built alongside the forge-master's house about 1804-6. (Another example was at Nantyglo (*page 16*) where the first ironmaster is said to have occupied the centre house himself). The modern main road separates the row from the site of the Varteg Forge, which worked for less than ten years (and then again only from 1823 to 1840). Isolation away from any other workings, and the lack of success prevented any expansion of either the works or the settlement. The row survived almost unaltered for 170 years and is now a 'listed' building. It is cared for by a private trust which intends to restore and furnish two houses for public exhibition.

John Street, Bethesda (Gwynedd) *SH 623 668* is not so much a street as a network of linked footpaths and alleyways. Covering a rocky outcrop behind the houses of the High Street, this little community is a fragment of the earliest unplanned part of the town, which was gradually developed in the 1820s. The irregular layout of houses of different types, the unfenced plots of land, the meandering unpaved footpaths, the many awkward junctions of buildings and changes of ground level, all bring to mind the description of Merthyr Tydfil in 1803. Today John Street is a fascinating survival, but with a little imagination its earlier more rugged character can be re-created.

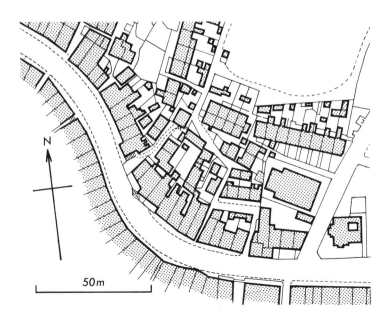

50m

In a few isolated cases, workers' houses were built around a geometric shape, such as a square or semi-circle, obviously following the ideas of Georgian planning for the well-to-do. Perhaps the most striking example of such a layout was the **Triangle** at **Pentrebach, Merthyr Tydfil** (Glamorgan) *SO 0596 0418*, on the cover of this booklet. It was built between 1840 and 1852 for the Plymouth Ironworks, and at the time of writing is, unhappily, derelict. Such planning, though, was always exceptional; if planned at all, most industrial housing was set out either in roughly parallel rows of houses all facing one way, or in streets, with houses built on plots on both sides of a carriageway.

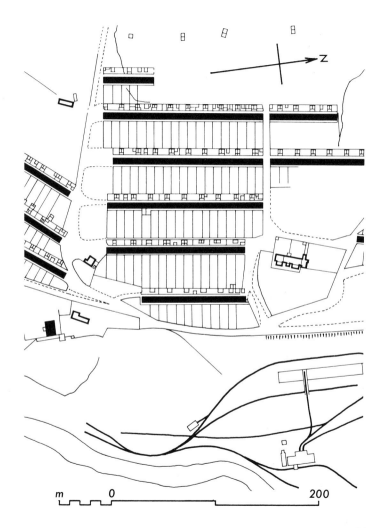

The Scotch Houses, Llwynypia, Rhondda (Glamorgan) *SS 992 932* were built from about 1865 onwards in connection with Archibald Hood's Llwyn-y-pia Colliery. Part of a development of more than 200 houses, often simply called 'The Terraces', they are a classic example of the parallel row layout in its final form. Each house faces westwards across the Rhondda valley. In front is its garden, behind is an access path about two-and-half metres wide at its maximum; a vehicle road climbs up the hillside, cutting across the ends of the terraces. With wide windows and sizeable private gardens, the houses offer accommodation of a much better quality than most workers could find or pay for in the large towns of Wales and England at that time. Like Stack Square, Blaenavon (*page 9*) they show that better housing was one of the accepted methods of attracting skilled labour to a developing area of new industry.

The street system of development is more suitable for wheeled traffic than the row system, but it seems unlikely that this was the main reason for the change from rows to streets. In the early industrial town wheeled traffic did not have the importance that it has today. Household necessities were delivered by horse and cart to the better-off members of the community, but the labouring classes could save some of their slender resources by carrying in what they needed for themselves. Retail street traders used hand-carts or ponies to carry their goods. The real advantage of the street layout was the flexibility that it offered to the builders of houses. Rows had to be developed in sequence (unfinished rows can be seen at the top and right of the plan on *page 51*), but plots bordering a street could be developed haphazardly. Once the streets had been set out, the land adjoining them could be divided into plots of any required size, and houses could be built at the pace which individual developers found convenient. The completion of a single street could take thirty years or more.

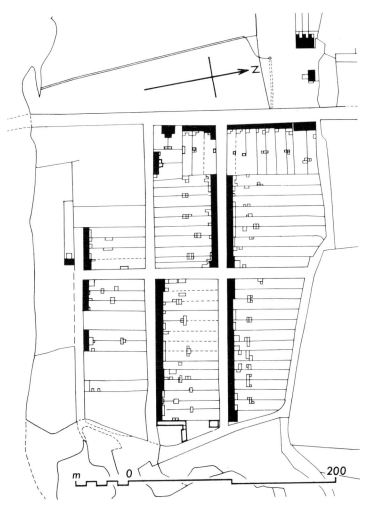

Most of **Pembroke Dock** (Dyfed) was laid out on the street grid system. The main street lines of the lower part of the town were fixed by 1818. In the separate suburb of East Pennar, laid out after 1841, very little of the street frontage was ever built up. The photograph shows houses in **Grove Street, East Pennar** *SM 964 022*. Such single-storey houses of the West Wales type (*compare pages 10 and 11*) were extensively used in the building of Pembroke Dock. Their roofs were often constructed of imported hardwood, which was presumably obtained from the dockyard where wooden warships were built and repaired.

The copper workers' settlement at **Tŷ-Maen, Cwmafan,** near **Port Talbot** (Glamorgan) *SS 788 925* is illustrated here by a photograph taken about 1900 and preserved in the collection of the Port Talbot Historical Society. The street layout probably dates from about 1848, when control of the Cwmavon copper works passed for a time to the Bank of England. Bethania Chapel at the far end of Pelly Street (centre) was erected in 1850 and the infant school on the opposite side of the same street was opened in 1855. Before the building of Tŷ-Maen, the copper workers' houses had been set out in scattered rows, some of which can be seen stretched out along the hillside in the background of this picture. But on a new flat site, a simple form of street grid was the obvious choice. A railway line runs through the middle of the settlement but otherwise there are no cross streets. Architecturally this scheme was as dour and utilitarian as The Ranks at Abercarn (*page 41*). The smelting company built its own houses to a design of forbidding appearance, using moulded blocks of black copper slag to form the surrounds of windows and doorways. Each house had four rooms, all of the same size like The Ranks, Abercarn. In 1976 more than half the settlement had been demolished and much of the remaining part was derelict.

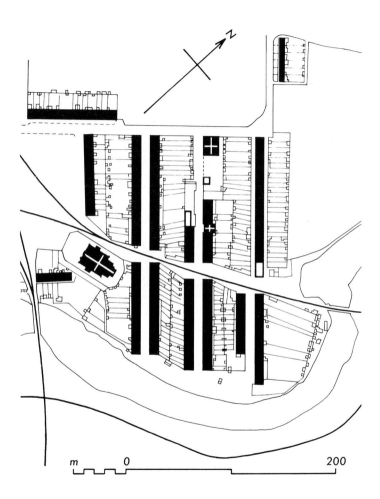

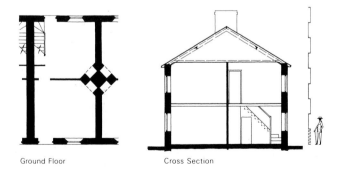

Ground Floor   Cross Section

Plantation Street, Rhymni (Glamorgan) *SO 1172 0686* was built between 1837 and 1841, after the amalgamation of the Union and Bute Iron Works into the Rhymney Iron Company. It was demolished in 1972. This picture illustrates a transitional stage in the formation of a street layout. Two rows were erected facing each other, rising gradually along a curving hillside. The slope at the side of the modern roadway shows that no attempt was made to bring the rows to the same level, which would have been necessary if a paved street had been planned originally. In 1842 Sir Edmund Head reported of this district "Very few, or none (of the houses) have privies. Sewerage is entirely unknown and the surface drainage is imperfect. There is a great accumulation of filth around the houses." (Poor Law Commissioners, *Local Reports*, London, 1842, 99). It is just possible to imagine this scene with the roadway replaced by an expanse of mud, dotted with heaps of dung and kitchen refuse.

Panton Place, Holywell (Clwyd) *SJ 1870 7577* was built in 1816 in the centre of the town for Paul Panton Jnr, the Sheriff of Flintshire. The date is picked out in darker bricks between the first floor windows. At that time Holywell was a centre of textile, metal and mining industry, close to the cultural influence of Liverpool, which in the late eighteenth century had become the largest provincial city in Britain. The elegant facades of Panton Place are decidedly 'polite' in character, rivalling the smaller houses of the time in Liverpool. Originally each house had four large rooms and a cellar. Alternate houses had an extra street door (now blocked) which led straight into the front room. Here the occupant, perhaps a trader or professional man, would have carried on his business. Visitors to the family used the other street door. In 1970 the interiors of all the houses were reconstructed by Holywell Urban District Council, to a design by the architects Brian Lingard and Partners, to make flats for elderly people.

Once a row housing scheme had been built, the number of houses could not be altered easily. Sometimes large row houses were later split into two; this happened at both Rhymni and Tredegar, as the prosperity of the ironworks there declined. But the street grid layout could be built up gradually to almost any density of dwellings, by filling in the land behind the street frontage with courtyard houses.

Baili-Glas Court, Twyn-yr-Odyn, Merthyr Tydfil (Glamorgan) *SO 0518 0584* does not possess the romantic charm of the scene on the page opposite. Most of the houses around it have been rebuilt, but the row on the left, which is almost identical with Gregory's Row (*page 22*), still shows something of its original character. The peeling surface of the wall reminds us of the days when houses were white-washed regularly with lime and tallow, building up a thick multi-layered coating as a protection against driving rain. Much of the area of Baili-Glas Court is now occupied by brick and asbestos cement sheds sheltering the outside water-closets and coal-houses which the original builders did not provide.

Pump Court, off **Commercial Street, Penygloddfa, Newtown** (Powys) *SO 1074 9191* was built about 1825 to 1830. It was reached by an archway through a row of back-to-back houses (*compare pages 24 and 27*), which gave access to the back houses of the row as well as to those in the court. The narrow two-room houses facing the court have large windowed living rooms suitable for textile industry outworkers. The pitched stone paving falling to a longitudinal gutter, the water tap with its drain, the brick *tŷ-bach* sheltering the outside water-closet, and even the makeshift ash-can, remind us of that quartet of sanitary necessities which play so large a part in the story of Victorian public health – surface drainage, uncontaminated drinking water, water-borne sanitation and refuse collection.

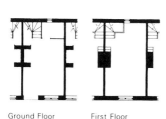

Ground Floor   First Floor

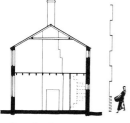

Cross Section

Some of the industrial towns of Wales have been so little altered that they are now recognised as classic specimens of nineteenth century town layout. **Bethesda** (Gwynedd) is one such town. Once absolutely dependent for its existence upon the Penrhyn Slate Quarries, Bethesda suffered greatly from the decline of the slate industry during and after the calamitous strike of 1900-02, and in its decline has preserved its original structure. On *page 49* the earliest unplanned centre of the town is shown. On these pages are two planned developments of later years.

The **Gerlan** estate *SH 632 664* with more than 100 plots for individual development was laid out in the summer of 1864. The layout and all the buildings were approved by the Commissioners appointed under the Bethesda Improvement Act of 1854, and their influence is visible today. The houses are ranged in straight rows, with roads of statutory width (21 feet), and regulation size access courts at the back of the houses. But the basic layout was not devised for the Commissioners; it can be traced to the older unregulated settlement of Rachub one mile to the north. The estate is divided into several sections; the two on the slope nearest to the camera in this view are both based on spine roads which run down the hillside at right angles to the rows of houses. Each section was planned separately; though the rows of houses appear to be continuous, the rear access courts did not join up and there was no planned connection between the two spine roads (except at the top of the slope by the chapel). As can be seen from the picture, the rows were further sub-divided into plots large enough for between one and four houses. The individual owners chose their house design and had it built, either separately or in partnership with their immediate neighbours.

Tan-y-Bwlch, Mynydd Llandegai (Gwynedd) *SH 600 654* with the other cottages on Douglas Hill, shows the ultimate development of model settlement as devised by the managers of the Penrhyn quarry. An area of the common waste on Llandegai mountain was enclosed, and fenced off into narrow plots of land, crossed by an even narrower access road. The plots were leased to quarry workers for thirty years, on condition they themselves built houses of an approved design. When the leases expired, houses and land reverted to the Penrhyn estate. The system was a notorious example of unbridled capitalist exploitation, yet the houses too are not without interest. Built during the 1870s they are lineal descendants of the traditional *croglofft* cottage (*page 10*). This basic design was taken up about 1790-95 by the Penrhyn estate agent, Benjamin Wyatt, made more regular in outside appearance and widely used for the early quarry housing. With successive improvements and enlargements it remained the favoured type for the next eighty years. Hundreds of houses of this kind can be seen in and around Bethesda. The same continuity applies to the plots of land attached to each house. Infertile and exposed though they are, they carry on the tradition of the part-agricultural, part-industrial way of life which was pursued fifty or a hundred years before by the weavers of Machynlleth and the lead-miners of Cwmystwyth.

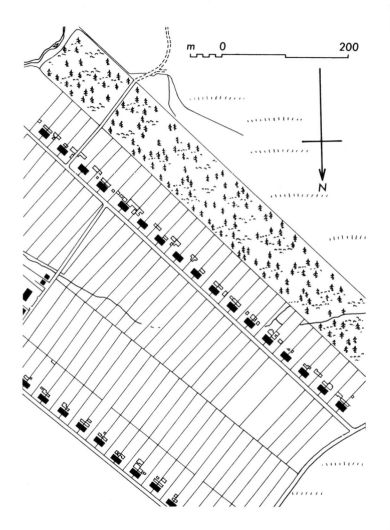

Postscript — 1985

The third printing of this booklet provides a chance to add a postscript to the original 1977 text. During the last 8 years public opinion has moved some way towards a greater appreciation of the interest and value of old houses. Derelict abandoned rows are no longer such a common sight in Wales and the uncertainties that hung over some of the houses illustrated here have mostly now been resolved, by either their demolition or their repair.

The most striking change has happened at Merthyr Tydfil, once the largest industrial town in Wales. Eight pictures of Merthyr Tydfil and Dowlais houses were chosen for this booklet and in 1977 five of these house groups were still standing. Now only one row, at Gellideg *(page 8)*, remains on its original site and its future is by no means certain. Six of the houses from Rhydycar *(page 28)* are being rebuilt at the Welsh Folk Museum, St Fagans, Cardiff. All the others have been demolished, including Cyfarthfa Row *(page 36)* which at one time had been selected for preservation. On the list of demolitions elsewhere are Penybryn *(page 10)*, Princess Street *(page 33)*, Bayliss Row *(page 37)*, the houses known as Blue Cottages at Aberllefenni *(page 43)* and Pump Court, Newtown *(page 59)*.

Fortunately some groups of houses have been preserved. Butetown *(page 40)* and Panton Place *(page 57)* were already secure in 1977. Rhydycar has been mentioned above. After many years of delay Stack Square *(page 9)* is being repaired for display. Forge Row, Cwmavon *(page 48)* has passed into the care of Torfaen Museum Trust. Three of the houses at Bunkers Hill, Bersham *(page 12)* also survive, and Brickfield Terrace, Machynlleth *(page 34)* has been restored to use. Most remarkable of all is the rebuilding of Jones Court, Cardiff *(page 23)* to become the offices of an architects' partnership. Elsewhere though the effects of modernisation have been less happy. External cement rendering and window replacement are the most common, and often the most damaging, of these changes. In this way Victoria Avenue, Llanidloes *(page 38)* and Chapel Street *(page 27)* and Union Street *(page 13)* in Newtown have lost some of their essential quality. Among larger groups of housing, such as The Scotch Houses *(page 50)* and Gerlan *(page 60)*, there have been many alterations.

The selection of pictures made in 1977 reflected what was then known about Welsh industrial houses. One important point has become more clearly evident since then. In the larger industrial areas, most of the house types had been identified in 1977 and subsequent demolitions have much reduced the variety of houses to be seen. But in the smaller country towns, and on the fringe of the old industrial areas, more early workers housing types have been recognised, some of which could well have been included in this booklet alongside the numerous examples from Glamorgan and Gwent. Such dwellings include: in Gwynedd, 2-4 Brick Street, Pentraeth, in Anglesey, and the quarrymen's village of Tre-forris, Cwmystradllyn: in Clwyd, Leicester and St Hilary's Terraces, both inside the town walls of Denbigh, Bank Place, Holywell and Brick Row, Hawarden*: in Powys, Mount Pleasant, Welshpool (dated 1824) and Rhiwlas Terrace, Llanfyllin*: in Dyfed, the weavers' houses of Drefach-Felindre, especially the row at Drefelin. As the caption to the picture of Bunkers Row, Blaenavon *(page 15)* implies, some of these houses may have a significance beyond the borders of Wales. They may be the only existing representatives of house types once common in the industrial towns of the rest of Britain and thus an important archaeological survival. So, though scope for the study of industrial housing has been reduced over recent years in the main industrial areas of Wales, there are still opportunities in our smaller towns and rural areas for the recognition and preservation of interesting working-class houses.

* Brick Row and Rhiwlas Terrace are both illustrated in the new companion to this booklet, *Welsh Country Workers Housing 1775-1875* (see note on inside front cover).